The Dirt Looks a Bit Different Now

by Melissa Crockett Meske

A New Poetry Collective

**First published in 2026 by
Melissa Meske Publications,
Macoupin County, Illinois U.S.A.**

ISBN: 979-8-9997541-9-6

First Edition

Designed for publication by

Melissa Crockett Meske

Cover design by Melissa Crockett Meske

**For more information about the author
and her published works,
visit https://macmeske.com/**

Where there is brokenness, there is an abundance of grace. ~ Unknown

This collection of works picks up where my first poetry anthology reached its ending. It features original poetry developed from 2016 to the start of 2026.

Thus, it is dedicated to all those who have continued to inspire and encourage me to keep creating visuals through words.

It is also dedicated to those who are out there in the world with a secret just waiting to be shared and a journey just waiting to be discovered. I hope the courage to share myself so personally on the pages ahead will help your voice emerge authentically and uniquely, sharing who's really you.

The past 10 years have been full of brokenness, but it is through the memories made that I have been able to still find the good. Writing these pieces helped me to move through all the grief and heartbreak and arrive where I am today. My personal drum circle has shown me so much grace all along my journey, and for that I am truly and forever grateful.

Being a published author is part of Melissa Crockett Meske's lifetime journey as a versatile communications professional.

"I have crafted hundreds of stories and thousands of words. I have also captured more storytelling images than I can honestly remember," Meske notes. "I am a published author, editor, journalist, writer, lyricist and photographer. You'll find my byline in publications all over the U.S."

During her years living in the Eastern Panhandle of West Virginia, Meske published her first poetry anthology, wrote a set of lyrics that were turned into professionally produced song, and edited four books for other authors.

The St. Louis Writers Guild published its 2024 Member Anthology, which included a narrative essay penned by Meske. More recently, on Nov. 1, 2025, Meske's first children's book debuted on Amazon: "LUNA THE CAT: She said that!"

A Hero Who Just Might Not Know

Since before I could ever remember
Or at least as far as I know
My mom has always been my hero
Despite all of the bumps in our road

She may not have always known this
Heroic is not something she would say
A life filled with luxury she has missed
But one with many good memories has stayed

She and I made so many together
One I remember so well from age five
Is of me opening up The Telegraph
And reading to her the stories inside

I know the day will come sometime
When she and I won't make them anymore
But we'll have so many to take with us
Like the one when my son slammed the door

My mom has always been my hero
Despite a life lived much harder than most
She has taught me to be the kind of woman
Who has substance, not just merely a ghost

A Journey Back Home

The water sprays over the rocks of the mountains
Each drop glistens like a diamond brilliant-cut
As the stream rushes under the train bridge
Moving fast like it has somewhere to be

Small patches of daffodils are blooming
Out in the wild along the rail's rugged path
They welcome us with their bright yellow faces
Bursting through tree lines that seem like they're dead

Soon the trees will just become black marks
Against the indigo blue sky of the night
Those trees will be the river's next victims
But setting roots free like the leaves in seasons before

A current of bodies now moves through Union Station
Floating along steady with an exact rapid stride
Swift not quite with the force of a tsunami
But more like the twist of a tornado at best

A Mellencamp Movement

The guitar chords strike first,
but soon the drum cadence joins in,
As the cymbals crash, the vocals begin.

Softer at first, because he's just a young boy,
Then louder as he asserts
The grander ideas behind his teenage joy.

In the background next rises the sounds of an organ
To premise the sermon for when he takes the stand
And declares to his girl, "I ain't talkin…" at least for then.

Hands clap to mark the beginning of something
That just hurts so good,
The drums all get louder; the guitar riffs follow suit.

Each time the word love is met with loud cymbals on cue,
As he answers the question "what hurts?"
And says, "Hey baby it's you…"

Inspired by John Mellencamp's Hurts So Good

A Resort in the Woods, Unlike Fairmont

One snowy evening I started writing
Anything but thoughts of promise and hope,
But the lonely shake of a harness bell
Brought me a new sound before then unknown.
Miles had always connected me to a darkness
I would have elsewhere encountered alone.
But now through the unmistaken still of the woods,
This beacon swept through the trees as they slept
And shimmered down on the frozen lake below.
Yet with the farmhouse still off in the distance,
Still further was the village we call home.
The sweeping wind eased through her downy mane,
Shaken inquisitively by my deep chestnut brown mare.
On this night, once said the year's darkest evening,
She wondered why we had even stopped here.

Inspired by Robert Frost's Stopping by Woods on a Snowy Evening

Another Saturday Night

Another Saturday night without you
Wanting so much to be in your arms
Knowing I'll be kept safe there
Knowing you'll keep me from harm

Wrapped in our own vulnerabilities
We breathe in each other's love at night
Then the morning sun rises
And your arms fall from my side

Do you feel as empowered as I do
With our resting spirits intertwined?
Futurespeak, life without you
Is something far from my mind

At the Bottom of the Hill

Quiet like the rain falling gently
On a mid-September afternoon,
I listen to the sounds of you breathing
As you lie next to me sleeping in our blue bedroom.

Nearly three years ago and six months before now
You walked down that hilly and brick-lined path,
And met me for the first time in the gallery
Real love would bloom from there at last.

And now as we grow old together
So too does our love mature.
But it never withers, fades or falters,
Because it's real, and therefore endures.

This life we now share at times can move slowly,
And sometimes just seems so damn hard.
But I still want to spend all the rest of our days together
And all the rest of our nights wrapped up in each other's arms.

Be the Light

I woke up yesterday morning
Unwillingly and too early to begin breathing it in
The sounds and the sights too eager to greet me
For I am a night owl, you see,
And once more life's challenges had managed
To keep Mister Sandman a safe distance from me
That knock, it had come too soon and too loudly

I woke up this morning
More willingly, quite ready to take it all in
Eager to greet all the things that were waiting
For my night's slumber reach its inevitable end
The sun warmed my face much more kindly
As I sat and wrote the words of this poem
Mister Sandman and I had swapped stories in
 Dreamland

Today came with a promised new challenge
Even as the neighbor once more started her day
As usual with her kids who must live with her yelling
Not even the whimpers of their sad puppy
Could even break me down still
The tree's white blossoms had stayed pretty,
 despite all of that noise
And the squirrel kept an eye on me closely as he
 scurried around in the blades

I think he was curious and just being playful
As he twitched his tail and seemingly laughed
Within the next moment I paused on my pages
My pencil stopped dead in its tracks
I closed my eyes, leaned my head back and soaked in the sun fully
Reflecting on each of the minutes as one by once they passed
Deciding once more to find the good in the challenge,
 once more in being a light

Biography Photography

An editorial written
With images of
The dislocation of societal values and goals
The natural impulses
That once brought
Her lens to a point blurring lines
Now striking
A divided-by-class
Poverty and wealth definitive, in contrast pose

Calm at the End of the Night

After the rain passes and the night slowly
Falls upon us, what will we do then?
Maybe we'll catch the glimpse of a rainbow
And once more search for that pot of gold
We have been told many times waits at its end

Or maybe we'll watch all the children
Gathering up the worms and the snails
As they play on the sidewalk, splashing
In the puddles, laughing, without a care in the world
While us mothers rush around to clean them up dry
We think back to our own moms and those yesterdays gone by

The sun has been at it for days now, shining down on us bright
Exhausted, it seeks refuge behind the clouds of the storm
The blades and the leaves all reach upward
To welcome what is falling down from the sky
As the wind takes its part in the action, in protest
The branches sway bravely before breaking away

Lightning takes on the role filled most often by sunshine
With claps of thunder its companion, it lights up the sky
But soon these storms will too slumber
And the clouds will give way to the night
As just like for millions of years before us
Millions of stars join together, singing a soft lullaby

Color of Windows

Each day begins with the color of teal in the window,
It is blue and green with some gray.
It delivers a message from those fighting violence,
And now shades the U.S. 100-dollar-bill.
Also linked with marine life and the Dolphins,
On the Desktop, my wallpaper is filled.

Contemplating the Verses of Life

Sheets that are soft but of platinum lie beneath me
Sunday afternoon spent composing from bed
The words at first whisper softly
As they move down my fingers and out of my head

Pages of ivory linen patiently await their arrival
After months of emptiness passing before
Marks quickly fill them up with definition
And the pages are lonely no more

Sometimes my pencil moves too slowly
Or maybe the words just come way too fast
Trying to capture all of life's stories
From the here and the now and the past

As a cool breeze blows across me through the window
The air carries the cardinal's song into our room
Causing me to shift all of my focus
To the comfortable love here still in bloom

I work to transcribe our true story
With a blushing red rose at its start
A tale of a thorn-wounded woman
And the white knight who captured her heart

We carefully pieced our family together
Two sons with brown eyes, a daughter with blue
Unsure of what all that could happen
Now another layer of this love I share with you

Conversations with an Old Friend

Old friend, what have you been up to?
What happened? Where have you been?
This world got so crazy without you
Or so it seemed every day since you had gone

I too have missed you during all of my absence
Despite the fact I had not actually drifted away
I was right here in the midst of your living
But in a life spent invisible for too long

You have fared far better than my wishes
My dreams were deterred and even stamped out
But now I have returned to your world to rebuild them
From where I had once drifted and ended up wrong

Old friend, it is so good to see you
I'm glad to know you are still around
We can forge from the stale and the oldness
A new bond that is authentic and strong

Cosmic Encounter: Harmony in Word

Lights of bright blue against the flatness of gray
Dark branches reach through the night sky
The clouds break open against the reach of the trees
A shower of stars, like droplets, cascade to the ground.

Just one tranquil moment to gaze upon it
As I rest against the stillness of the cold black ground
The landscape awakens from darkness to bright
My eyes consider the contrast, my spirit revels in its enlight.

Visions of color surround my periphery
But the subtleness of its hue keeps me quiet at rest
As my mind considers it attraction, my spirit's propelled
From its shadows once more to what I know I can do.

"Reach up toward the sky, let the clouds part away
The stars, they wait for you to join them.
Step into the circle with an eye focused upward
Toward forever, you will always see the blue in the sky."

Too many times over I've been told in my life
To stay out of that forest which endangers and swallows us all
But the trees that stand there against the wind and the years,
Are they not resolute as they stand, struggling to thrive and survive?

Can those same trees provide me shelter and strength
As I move on, anchored against the batter of life's storms?
As I let the words of my past rain down and transform me
Against the gray sky, a star of bright blue shines once more.

Eight Years: A Long Goodbye

I was always there
Until it became too much.
Too much for you to bear.

Too much for you
To turn your eyes
And find me standing near.

You said you'd be good,
You pleaded to just go home.

You said you were tired,
Tired of being tired.
And tired of being alone.

You said you would miss me.
You said you would miss us all.
You begged, you cried.

You took your last breath,
And then you died.

Now you're no longer alone.
You made it back home,
Love is again right by your side.

A final resting place for you now,
With your life's lasting moments,
Now mere dates chiseled in stone.

Yet, as I walk away with great pause,
Sadness does cloak me, but also, a sigh.

For Them and For Me

It's been years since the grief began
For the other eight in our fold.

But for me, it has ended a journey
Through a predation that began
Nearly two score and four years ago.

Reflecting upon his death, they recall
A sweet man, a best friend, a mentor.
My memories are in stark contrast to that,
With betrayal and untrust keeping score.

They all talk of an honorable man
Who offered them unconditional love and pride.

But to me, he gave nothing more than
A fragile life left unprotected,
And a never-ending need to hide.

Many relationships have since faltered
Without a proper compass to guide me.
The man who should have defined it long ago,
Instead shattered the template so defiantly.

Friday Night at the Theater

The actor's pace warms up the floor polish
Fueled by fright they hope to abolish
Before Friday night at the theater

The stage is an old set rebuilt just last week
New too: the sound cloud and black duvetyne
For Friday night at the theater

A small town of the past has since flourished
Its once rural legacy, now culture nourished
Each Friday night at the theater

It's not yet as crowded as it should be
The audience is not yet refined as it will be
On Friday night at the theater

Haiku: Along the Trail

The trail leaves nothing
But quiet inspiration
All along our path

Chilly afternoons
Spent on the trail together
Discovering us

We stop on the trail
Distant knocks on a tree heard
Holes are spied later

Us exploring life
On the Appalachian Trail
Finding each other

The miles of dirt
We travel onto today
Stillness for our souls

Marks to lead the way
White and blue blaze on the trail
Simpler terms than life

Haiku: Four

A desire for
Glorious places around
In my childhood

Simple touches shape
A reflection on our world
Time never embraced

A dream about love
A shelter my family
Hellbent to erase

One simple journey
A vision for my future
Empty if embraced

Haiku: In Season

Storms and floods surround
Thunder fills the sky with sound
Lightning strikes abound

Yesterday's storms pass
Destruction left behind
Those memories, gone

The snow falls softly
Billowy white flakes touch down
Like nature's gentle kisses

A new season blooms
In shades of yellow and red
Hope springs forth boldly

Warm sunbeams, blue sky
School is out, the children shout
Roses in full bloom

Crisp air, leaves tumble
Yellow, orange, brown in hue
Crinkle and crumble

Legacy of a Lifetime: A Mother's Love

A dozen red roses and a red tin foil heart
To show how much I still love you, and miss you,
And how much you stay in my thoughts

Each day goes by with me here and you gone
It seems like just yesterday
We walked through here, arm in arm

Why did it all happen the way that it did?
Why did all those demons
Have to take over your mind and clutter your head?

We had big plans of time we'd spend in the sun
Then your thoughts became fractured and lonely
As your mind came undone

Now I'm left to wonder, when this finally happens to me,
Who will I turn into, and who will I leave lonely?

Yes, I am lonely without you, despite loved ones all around
Each day I strive to be stronger like they want me
But comfort, often promised, is still yet to be found

The flowers that bloom as the birds fly on by
Are a different kind of beautiful now
In my altered view and through a teary eye

The barred owl's call is clear against the midnight moon
They say her call is about who's cooking
But really, I think she's asking about you

I've surrounded my emptied world and that void you used to fill
With things that once made your eyes sparkle, your soul smile,
Worldly goods left here to glitter and shine still

You passed the torch, joyful memories part of my journey now,
I'm doing as best I can each day,
Though still not quite that ready nor still not quite sure how

I do this in your memory, to honor those things you loved most
Traditions of love shared forward by you first and me now
With my mind left to serve as your legacy and host

Lost But Still Searching

A wanderlust stirs inside the young gypsy
As a call comes from deep down inside
And she gazes once more at the city
She knows she may never again find

Basic instinct keeps moving her forward
An awareness that she needs to survive
But still she is weak with a hunger
That can only be nourished in her mind

Moments on this live track keep her naked
Creativity unexposed due to pride
Instead of cloaked in the robes made of satin
That can only be displayed with their kind

Determined to regain her focus
Still a vessel trapped far from the tribe
She fascinates herself as life's witness
Like wildfire the images burn in her eyes

Lost in Love

Taking part in relationships
Hiding behind a shield of another's love
No need to love myself, in part or in whole

Self-love comes with doubt as to how or why
I don't know who she is, or what about her
Would garner such love worthy or apropos

Unconsciously from her I've moved quite far
Loving others without question, even those still unmet
Yet selfishly a love of who I am, I can no longer show

Embarking on a sacrificial journey so others feel love
With and for themselves happy, ergo with or for me no

Meanwhile along the path I keep waiting
For that golden ticket, that golden buzzer's sound
Hopeful for one person to help recover and begin to regrow

That chanceful one person to love me enough to say
I believe in you and your dreams, *we* got this, and then
To tirelessly guide her back down the path that she now needs to go

I cry a little each day in mourning as I watch others living
Amidst dreams all on their own, as they emit such an outward glow
Inside I wonder who or what it is they have come to know

Moments Managed

In the blink of an eye life changes
At least that is what the experts advise
Even more so if you do things without thinking
Living the days one at a time
There are those who must plan each moment
Structure keeps their lives clearly defined
Still others are fine in that moment
Without a mandate to serve as their guide
As for me I prefer to be efficient
Working hard to maximize all of my time
But with a daily schedule that is ignited
By the creative sparks of my spontaneous mind

Mortality Musings at Midnight

Maybe in the next life
I'll spend less time inside my head
Focusing on the good all around me
With more time spent on self-care instead

Maybe in the next life
I'll have a kinder, gentler spirit
One that is warm and welcoming
And a softer voice so no one will ever fear it

Maybe in the next life
I'll spend less time avoiding and analyzing
Rather, embrace the new and the different
No judging others for life choices, or criticizing

Maybe in the next life
We all can try a little bit harder
To build an accepting world of kindness
And enjoy the life we're given without being a martyr

Moving On: A Cento

The meadowlark's song greets the sunrise
As I look up toward the morning sky.
It is a perpetual blue; the clouds, all silver lined.

A glimmer of hope fills its boundaries.
But soon the butterflies and roses will sleep,
As life's seasons quickly rush by.

The fireflies and town lights now cast a faint glow
Against the lonely darkness of night.
Look closely, can you still see me, or have we already goodbye?

A cento is a poem made entirely of lines from other poems. The name comes from the Latin word meaning a cloak made out of patches. The cento differs from found poetry in that every line is taken from another poem, instead of just any borrowed material. Here, I have utilized lines and fragments from other poetic works of mine.

Night by the Campfire

The silent sounds of darkness
Surround us, envelop us,
As summer embers crackle and fall.
Splitting through the night's quietness,
The cry of the lonesome train call.

Sparkling spectators standing skyward
Watch down on us as we intrude
Upon the owl's own hunting ground.
In the distance, the reality of a life,
Come Monday, to which we are bound.

The frogs and cicadas shout back at us,
Telling us to vacate their peaceful home.
To leave their sacred space far behind us
And return to the monotone vacancy
Of the world of which we all know.

On a Tuesday in July

In the still of the rain
I hear no sweet song of the summer bird.
Once steadfast and sure against the bright summer sun,
'Tis only the trees and the cool stormy breeze
That now continues to converse with me.

Showers, they come softly,
Then they go, only to visit again later,
As does the tap, tap, tap that makes up the dance
Of the returning raindrops' descent
Once more onto the songbird's stage.

Tightly woven orange balls
Of curled up tiger lilies line the gravel drive,
Sharply contrasting against the misty whitewash
Of the showering rain and the lush summer-green grass.
The tree frog belts out a cautious, yet confident one-note tune.

But the one thing I notice most
Among the straight-down gravitational falls,
The wind-bent limbs and the moist green blades
Is a loss of beauty in this moment's voice.
The songbird's silence stays against the still of the rain.

On the Shelves of the Shop in Old Town

I walk through this eclectic shop inquisitively,
Hopeful the discovery of my real history waits somewhere inside.
Repeatedly exploring the shelves and pathways,
In search of something to call out and capture my eye.

My attention, by means of my pocketbook,
Leads me to revisit each corner and piece.
The shelves display lost memories of families,
Generations of people whose lives have gone long by.

Is it pressed into that set of German saucers with raised borders
That once upon a time might my great grandparents have owned?
Or perhaps in those crystal sunflower-carved servers
That seven decades earlier had their stories forged inside?

Many treasures could piece the lines of my past together,
Including the two discoveries I'm already taking home.
But none quite as bold as the third tells its preface;
My mom's childhood, this vase of pink glass tries to disguise.

Recalculating

The sun has gone down on the days together,
Now the evenings pass with us each alone.
Surrounded by a million stars in the darkness,
I miss you and all the things I have known.

I wandered off the path for a moment,
And followed a broken compass for too long,
Now travel on the path of what was once our journey,
Without you is not where I belong.

I am strong, so much stronger
Than on that day from our travels I detoured.
With or without you I know I can make it,
But alone is not what I preferred.

The sights and sounds of the world envelop me.
The bells in the tower, muffled, still gently toll.
The birds sing a soft lullaby for all who listen.
The tree frogs sound as enchanting as with you, I recall.

Yet all I hear clearly is my own heartbeat,
In unison with yours nevermore.
Without you I move on, but more slowly,
Than the days I spent not missing you before.

Relevant, or Relic?

Relevant or relic?
My mind's debate.
Am I just an illusion?
Beyond my "best by" date?

I still have much to offer
Decades of learning to give
I can tell you my life's proper
And make yours easier to live

It wasn't that long ago
When you asked me to share
The things that I know
To make life's lessons easier to bear

Yet each night I cry out
With quiet tears that I bear
As witness, my silent shout:
Does anyone even care?

Lonely, restless and older
I no longer fulfill a need
A solo gig has unfolded
Where once, we were a team

Relevant or relic?
What is my current state?
Was my relevance a delusion?
A life planned together, displaced?

Shades of Time: Golden, or Gray?

Why do they call these years golden
When they are clearly defined in gray?
Silver tones come in and take over,
And despite our best efforts, they stay.

Golden, these are the best years of our lives?
Then why do our bones ache,
Our teeth break, and our hands shake
As daily new obstacles continue to arrive?

Flecks of gray, first to come as we progressively age.
A few years later, streaks of silver begin to dominate,
Taking over all the signs of our younger days.
And with each year, the streaks of silver take on a whiter shade.

A golden celebration after 50 years of wedded bliss.
I'm okay with this kind of shimmer if we ever get to this.
A silver celebration after 25 years, this I can do too.
But living long into our golden years, who's really kidding who?

Golden, or gray, depends on one's own perspective.
A golden shimmer or hue brings forth feelings of a warm sun.
While gray, distinguished or unruly, has a different objective:
A beautiful snow white, or the slow mark of someone's undone?

Shaken, and Unsure

A leader who can't find her footing
Despite beneath, the solid ground.
Shadowed by those before her
Where loyalties are still bound.

Feeling more like a poser
Than someone has earned this.
Well trained in all the motions
Yet foreign still are the footsteps.

I don't think I belong here
Despite working for this my whole life.
Confidence now replaced by fear
I no longer permeate a sense of pride.

How do I go back to where I was before?
Once filled with vision and aspiration,
The walls of society's education
Have since fractured me at my core.

In my own element I sense that I am worthy.
My own individuality is on parade.
At my desk or in the classroom
I am a force unafraid.

Why can't I be worthy of this walk,
Trekking well beyond my predecessors' path?
This journey was meant too for my travels.
My soul has provided its map.

Maya, Ruth, Kamala and Michelle.
Amelia, Miss Meda, my friend's mom Jackie as well.
All are beacons that still light up the trail.
A trail to propel us all forward without falter
Rising up to a place where we lead without fail.

Six Words: Life Forever Changed

- *Who are you??* It's me, Mom…
- The small coffins are the heaviest.
- Alexa, delete Mom from my contacts.
- Strangers, friends, best friends, lovers, strangers.
- I met my soulmate. She didn't.
- An only son, a folded flag.
- *'Just married'* read the shattered windshield.
- Ever seen chalk lines that small?
- It's our fiftieth. Table for one.
- The fire was out of control.
- Married. I've never felt more alone.
- The test results came back positive.
- He said he loves you. Finally.
- War is over. They're coming home.
- You're hired. Welcome to the company!
- Best wishes for your well-deserved retirement.
- She's safe; no injuries were found.
- Seasons change: A beautiful spring arrives.
- Sunbeams have broken through the clouds.
- Birds are singing, bees are buzzing.

So I've Been Told

Bittersweet are the memories of days spent together
Empty nostalgic feelings dominate most of them all
Poignant are the pictures that were taken
Some black-and-white, some in color
All faded and fuzzy inside old frames
The years they were cherished long gone

One is from when we were still family
Dad's on the end, Mom's on the other
Two rows of kids in between them, all smiling
Each one of us with our favorite toy
Five girls and four boys, full of happiness
Back before it all went all wrong

A misty fog lies over most of my visions
Of how life was all together back then
I was so small and the youngest
Most of my life was shaped by later events
With those visions much more vivid
Of the life we all lived at the end of their song

I know we shared great moments together
In those earliest years of my life
I've been told about all of those good times
I just wish I could feel them all
Perhaps then I could stop drifting
And understand better where it is I belong

Soft

A soft feather floated
Across a cerulean, blue sky
It sliced through the billows
Of soft clouds piled high

The feather was white
With just a touch of gray
Abreast on the breeze
Of that soft summer day

As it floated and swirled
And cut through the blue
It caught up with the butterfly
And soft memories of you

With a border edged white
And a fine black line too
The butterfly's wings dotted orange
Were filled in a soft powdery blue

The feather brushed lightly
As the resting butterfly again flew
And I thought to myself, softly,
What a beautiful place, here with you.

Sparkling Stars, Silver Moon

The moon fills the late-night sky
With a cool and welcoming yellow light
As billions of stars sparkle and shine
Against the darkness way up high.

A few wispy, stretched clouds
Float across the moonlit horizon
Magical moments, reborn for a time,
Against the sparkling stars, enlivened.

The stars that have nothing to do but sparkle,
Just like the glow of the silver moon,
All that the heavens hold and offer
Brings me back to lost visions of you.

I've always loved the starry sky,
Lit up by the glow of a silver moon.
The beauty of the heavens, in harmony now,
Yet pale against memories reviewed.

Spring: Green

The color of renewal,
The color of hope and new life.
At first it seems muted by yellow,
But with growth its hue bursts through bright.
A sign of good health,
It is symbolic of wealth.
Full of energy, it breeds forth natural light.

The Art of Survival

Don’t let the art die with the artist
Be sure you first discover its muse
It is our task to recall it and remember as
Another death fills the streams of its news

Don’t let the art die with the artist
Fill instead each classroom with its songs
The wonder of each transformation
To the next ones we pass it along

Don’t let the art die with the artist
The world needs its beauty to survive
Without it there will be no passion
Without it we can’t understand the sunrise

Even without the piece’s creator
It must forever grow and be nourished
Humanity needs it to tell all its stories
The artist may be gone, but the work must still flourish

Don’t let the art die with the artist
The efforts must not after all be in vain
Journal pages to tell of the labors and toils
Each masterpiece painted with the beauty of the rain

The Best of My Childhood Memories

When I was just a little girl
I was happy with whatever we had
My Big Wheel, my Audrey, my pillow
Life really wasn't all that bad

With four brothers, four sisters
I am the youngest of nine
Our home, with all of those people
Quiet moments were often lost in time

My mom cooked for our army
A meal at the dinner table together each night
I never knew how much she struggled
Or the loneliness she harbored inside

When we moved up north to the new town
Only half of us still lived at home
It was there on the playground at my new school
When I first learned about how we were known

That dark-haired girl from the east side
Made fun of my sister and me every day
Although we lived on the west side
She laughed as she pushed me away

Her pink dress with bows came from Penney's
My outfit a hand-me-down or maybe Goodwill
So sad that she was that shallow and lonely
Meanwhile with love my heart had been filled

My family is now scattered and rather broken
The last four decades or so have been hard
But the best memories from my youngest of childhood
Still linger on the bike track in our back yard

The Dirt Looks Different Now

The dirt looks a bit different these days
Now that Mom has too come to stay.
At first it was unsettled, a kind of a crumbled gray.
Now grass is overhead but grown up a different way.

I wasn't ready for life without you
Even though I knew there'd come a day.
None of us live forever,
At least that's what other folks say.

Truth be told, as I too grow old,
My beliefs travel a separate way.
Of heaven or hell, neither I'm sold.
Rather as stars in the sky, we stay.

Your memory and lessons still guide me,
But not in the way you'd want me to pray.
Belief in a higher power? Perhaps.
But through nature is how I reflect and obey.

Loved ones, recent or long since passed by,
All still seen each day gathered 'round.
They live on, in my mind and in the sky,
Certainly not beneath the dirt on the ground.

The Grass is Just Grass

Sometimes I let myself daydream about how
I might have been viewed
I think of all the places I would have visited,
all the things I could do
If I had just listened to my heart instead of
following a clouded review
This life I am now living would resemble
nothing like that of the truth

We think the grass is much greener if we
can just get to the other side
Once we learn better, we protect ourselves
under a cloak of foolish pride
We keep plastering that fake smile on when
all we want to do is hide
"The grass is just grass," to my mom I
now finally confide

That grass felt cool and refreshing beneath
my bare feet at the park
The rose and meditation garden: they both
once fueled my creative spark
800 miles from somewhere, most evenings
now spent alone in the dark
It was nearly three years with the new grass,
yet left barely a mark

The mountains are intrusive reminders
as they invade our view
Of all the miles between us and those we
love, each and every one of you
*Chin up, stay focused—good things will
happen soon*
This is my mantra as I journey onward, still
seeking a shiny new source for a muse

The History of Happiness

Tulips, the crocus, and daffodils
Balloons, confetti, and pie
Lemonade, the Cardinals, and cardinals
Days that have long since passed us by

Guitars, music, and dancing
Voices lifted together in song
Swing sets, bicycles, and movies
Back before the family was divided and gone

Friends on the playground and field trips
Cave trips, road trips, and those first kisses
The roller rink, cartwheels and backflips
Ice cream, catching fish and the near misses

True love, our first home, and a byline
The children, grandchildren, and a song
Books and the words trapped inside them
Stories tell of our happiness, whether right or wrong

The Tree with White Blossoms

On this warm spring afternoon
I stare out the window
Next to the desk in my home office
The corner office with a view
The view, mostly being of asphalt
But a row of budding trees lines the hillside

From outside the panes and to the right
Of the corner that rises past three stories high
One tree stands forth quietly, making its annual debut
Its limbs are cloaked in white blossoms
A beautiful distraction for me and the bumblebee
In stark contrast to the canvas of cars and of black

The Trees No Longer Need Their Leaves

The trees no longer need their leaves,
So they drop them and let them go.
Just as the incandescent bulb
Releases its hold on the ambient light inside.

Both share their discards and spoils
So that another might benefit anew
From what remains useful and good.

Benefactors inject them with wisdom
From the world they have come to know.
Redefining and evolving with purpose renewed,
The fractures, once broken, now cautiously heal.

Isn't that what the circle of life is after all?

Inspired by "Leaves" by Maggie Smith

The Unintentional Bloom

Her lips were painted a bright orchid
As when the purple has come bursting through
Which is to say they were not painted orange or yellow
As when the epiphyte might otherwise develop its hue
And travel far from its Brazilian biome
As when the seeds made their first debut
Through Georgia O'Keefe's canvas and her subliminal view

Today is the Color of Blue

Number 1-8-3-7 by Pantone
Envisioned like that done by Tiffany
Defined a light-medium robin's egg blue

It is not quite the sky nor the periwinkle
But more like the softness invoked by the powder
My most favorite of all of its hues

Blue skies filled with puff clouds all day
Same sky the stars light up at each midnight
In Memphis it plays its own tune

Dark, light or bright, blue is loyal
Tranquil and calm as it visits the beachfront
Peaceful with purpose, it soothes

Trapped

Trapped. I feel trapped.
But not only by this world of isolation.
Too, my own fears and shortcomings.
I am trapped by my own hesitations,
The anxiety inside just keeps humming.

Somewhere there is strength.
The ability to come forth bold.
I've done it previously many times over;
A braveness beforehand awaits to unfold.

Age is its own trapping;
Another layer of bait as we grow old.
But as long as I can remember to do so,
I still have moments of love to behold.

I could look at them too as world trappings,
After all, love comes with isolation, hesitation, and fright.
Instead, I'll see love, and aging, as a life that was happy.
A spirit fulfilled, with the person who knew the best of me
Spending each day of life's journey trapped inside.

Undefined Journey

Just off the well-traveled path
I rest on a bench to the left
Of the lesser-known trail.
The birds sing bedtime lullabies
All around me, as the sun heads west;
Its warmth begins to pale.
I did not plan to make this journey;
Today I had other things I had to do.
But something propelled me forward;
A calling, from a voice that sounded like you.
I wasn't ready to talk about it:
The absence I feel inside.
I'm still angry and heartbroken;
You left me alone when you died.
"Life is, then life was," you noted,
As if that would make me feel better.
"How will you leave yours behind?"
Tugging closed the two sides of your old sweater,
I replied, *"I don't want to leave a legacy undefined."*
Thus, drives my journey, across each line of a page.
I hope my words can help mark my life travels;
Words to act like cairns on the path to my grave.

Wanderlust Turns in a Day

We wander down picturesque streets
Past plantations built centuries before.
Their landscapes are filled with old gardens,
Antebellum structures define Southern charm.

Sweet tea and mint juleps are offered,
We partake as we meander on by.
Magnolia trees are spilling their blossoms,
We notice the intoxication their fragrance invites.

But then we arrive to that spot at Fort Sumter
And a whole different scene fills the air.
We both want to move in much closer,
With stillness we consider what happened there.

When We Were Still Family

I remember that one summer day
Spent by the lake not far from home.
All my brothers and sisters were there,
At least that's as best I recall.

Mom and Dad were still married then,
And it seemed like they were in love.
My sister was big with their grandson,
But for now, I was still the smallest of all.

My memories of those good times and days
Have faded as the years passed us by,
So much happened to cast a dark shadow
Over the catch my brother-in-law made of that ball.

Mom always made the best fried chicken;
I remember we fought over the drumsticks and thighs.
I ran the bases for her and my big sister,
Because if I didn't, those two might just fall.

www.ingramcontent.com/pod-product-compliance
Lightning Source LLC
LaVergne TN
LVHW090618110826
845146LV00001B/443

* 9 7 9 8 9 9 9 7 5 4 1 9 6 *